BLoCkoLoGy

AN OffBEAT
WALKing guide
to LOWer
manHATTAN

written and
illustrated by

ROBERT JAY KAUFMAN

Turning Corners Press
PO Box 470628
Brookline Village, MA 02447
www.turningcornerspress.com

First edition 2005
Printed and bound in England by Butler and Tanner Ltd, Frome

Book design by Wilcox Design, Cambridge, MA
Map illustration by Mary Reilly Graphics

ISBN 0-9764188-0-0

LCCN 2004195048

Library of Congress Cataloging-in-Publication Data
Blockology: An Offbeat Walking Guide to Lower Manhattan.
Includes index.
1. Manhattan (New York, NY)-Guide-books
2. New York (NY)-Description
3. New York (NY)-Caricatures and collages

To Susan and Emili for their unwavering support,
and to my parents, Eleanor and Felix.

CONTENTS

ACKNOWLEDGEMENTS

I especially want to acknowledge the residents of Lower Manhattan, who engaged me in conversation, while I researched *Blockology* on foot. These instant urban acquaintances from all walks of life added immeasurably to my understanding of blocks and neighborhoods. I am most grateful that they freely shared their stories, local gripes, and pride in being New Yorkers.

As I searched for clues to best describe in writing the essential quality of a block, I discovered that one topic always led to another in rapid succession. Geography led to history that led to notable figures to politics to sociology to economics to architecture and so on, a continuous trail of influences. Seeing the connections among the influences has been made far easier because of the writings and principles of Jane Jacobs (*The Death and Life of Great American Cities*), Ada Louise Huxtable (*Classic New York*), Bernard Rudofsky (*Streets for People*), and Edmund Bacon (*Design of Cities*). They have dramatically influenced the way we all look at cities and helped launch the preservation movement in the 1960s. Since that time, special credit must be given to the efforts of the New York City Landmarks Preservation Commission, The Village Historical Society, and the many organizations of Volume: Voices of Lower Manhattan. This list would not be complete without mention of the many Lower Manhattan block associations that have tenaciously safeguarded the quality of urban life.

I owe a considerable debt to the following authors who thoroughly explored and documented the marvelous history of New York City: Kenneth T. Jackson and a host of contributors (*The Encyclopedia of New York City*), Edwin G. Burrows and Mike Wallace (*Gotham: A History of New York City to 1898*), Luc Santé (*Low Life*), Jane Mushabac and Angela Wigan (*A Short and Remarkable History of New York City*), James Trager (*The New York Chronology*), Eric Homberger (*The Historical Atlas of New York City*), and Henry Moscow (*The Street Book: An Encyclopedia of Manhattan's Street Names and Their Origins*). Wonderful public resources included the Ottendorfer Branch of the New York Public Library, the Web site for the Museum of the City of New York, and the Public Library of Brookline, Massachusetts.

Walking guides and maps of New York City provided vital information not only for on-site research, but also through virtual-walking in the confines of my studio. These marvelous works celebrate the architectural breath of the city and were invaluable in writing *Blockology*. They include *AIA Guide to New York City* (Norval White and Elliot Willensky), *New York: A Guide to the Metropolis* (Gerard R. Wolfe), *The Lower East Side: A Guide to Its Jewish Past in 99 New Photographs* (text by Ronald Sanders and photographs by Edmund V. Gillon, Jr.), *The Only Complete Guide to Greenwich Village* (Bruce Cranor Gaylord), *One Thousand New York Buildings*, (photographs by Jorg Brockmann and text by Bill Harris), *New York Songlines* (Jim

Naureckas at nysonglines.com), and *Manhattan Block by Block: A Street Atlas* (John Tauranac). In addition, *The Old Way of Seeing* (Jonathan Hale), and *Here Is New York* (E.B. White) through radically different means, brought clarity and poetry to a stroll down a city block.

The making of a book is largely a collaborative effort, first through much-needed encouragement in the idea stage. Amanda Bereny, Ken Clare, Kim Gordon, Al and Alice Kaufman, Karen Lewis, Ivan Majdrakoff, and Ramona Newton were readily available for sound advice. The publication of *Blockology* would not have been possible without the extensive participation of my wife, Susan Scott, who contributed mightily in all things involving *Blockology.* Craig Southard was invaluable for his support, suggestions, and many contributions, including an outstanding Web site design. Edward Campion edited the manuscript with insight and surgical precision. His curiosity and excitement for the subject matter was inspirational. Jean Wilcox oversaw the book design with vision and creativity.

This project was made possible by a sabbatical leave from The Art Institute of Boston at Lesley University and through the wonderful support of my colleagues and students, for which I am most grateful.

EVERY STEP

During the summer and autumn of 2003, I walked all 1,544 blocks[1] below 14th Street in Lower Manhattan. That means every step through the Gansevoort Market District, Greenwich, West and East Villages, Union and Hudson Squares, the Lower East Side, NoHo, NoLita, SoHo, TriBeCa, Little Italy, Chinatown, Civic Center, the Bowery, Fulton, Battery Park City, and the World Trade Center to the tip of the Financial District. I took my time. Why? Because I felt an inescapable connection to this remarkable place and wanted to know it better, not just well, but deeply.

A NAME IS LOST

My journey is one that starts with my Russian Jewish ancestors on both sides, who as immigrants settled in Lower Manhattan in the late 1880s. The name *Kaufman* is a gift from an immigration official, and as today's Manhattan White Pages attests, I am not alone. Nevertheless, our original family name is lost, so my history as a Kaufman begins in the Lower East Side. My grandparents and parents, uncles, aunts, and cousins have long since spread throughout the neighborhoods of Manhattan, to the outer boroughs and beyond into the suburbs in all directions. I was from the New Jersey contingent, and my father commuted everyday by train and ferry to his office at *2 Broadway*. Thankfully, a few of my aunts and uncles remained in Manhattan, and their apartments served as the center of our larger family gatherings. These were noisy reunions that not only celebrated our bond to one another but to the city itself. New York was always at the heart of our raucous conversations concerning politics, culture, entertainment, and, of course, food.

AMONG STRANGERS

From my earliest memories, I was in love with the visual complexity and diversity of Manhattan, the architecture, character, and frenetic pace. At my mother's side, I watched and listened to how she conversed with New Yorkers—waiters, bus riders, elevator operators, taxi drivers, butchers, policemen, and just about anyone within earshot. They freely shared their stories, and she loved the repartee. As a teenager, I explored the city's neighborhoods with my best friend, while taking full advantage of the then-cheap balcony seats on Broadway, visits to museums, and Yankee games. Why anyone would ask a thirteen-year-old for directions is still a mystery, but it happened to me a great deal. I thought it an honor, an important adult responsibility thrust upon me. When I didn't know the answer, I would ask someone nearby, and suddenly there would be a crowd enthusiastically discussing the best way to find someplace. As a result, New York never appeared to me as a cold and impersonal place, and I embraced the challenge of knowing the best way to get from point A to point B. At the time, I did not fully appreciate how these interactions with the public would affect my life. Curiously, years later I met the woman, who would become my wife, when she asked me for some information in the Port Authority Bus Terminal.

---

1. By my count, blocks with consecutive cross streets, not an official tally, but in the ballpark.

URBAN LIVING

From the 1930s through the 70s, it is well known that the nation's cities, with New York at the top of the list, were crumbling from an eroding tax base from huge shifts in the population caused by an exodus to the suburbs. Meanwhile, in Lower Manhattan, the textile traders in SoHo and TriBeCa were experiencing hard times. These small firms now only occupied the first floors in a sea of six-story cast-iron buildings. Landlords were desperate to rent spaces on the vacant floors above and found willing artists interested in low rents to transform these commercial properties into residences and studios. When I moved to TriBeCa in Lower Manhattan from San Francisco in 1977, one could not find a more desirable neighborhood in which to live. Life in that community of artists completely redefined my perception of what an urban neighborhood should be. For in those days, TriBeCa was nearly devoid of services, with few groceries, pharmacies or laundries. In fact, when cab drivers pulled up to our front door, they would ask in disbelief, "Does anyone live here?" Those of us who did live in those commercial lofts would radically change the face of Lower Manhattan and the city itself. New York City returned to its former glory quite simply because the people who loved it began to use it and enjoy it again.

IF SIDEWALKS WERE TRAILS

In fact, the city became so popular that I could no longer afford to live there. So it was on to Hoboken, New Jersey, and its view of Manhattan, where I resided for over a decade in another close community of artists and musicians. A position as a college art professor would lead my family and me to move first to Charlotte, North Carolina, and then to Boston. As the years passed, my affection for the urban scene grew stronger, and it inspired what I read and created artistically. The rough idea for this walking chronicle predates the events of 9/11; however, that tragedy only hastened my return to New York City. It was then that I decided to walk every single block in Lower Manhattan. A year later, I set out from a sublet studio apartment on Avenue A and East 2nd Street with a camera and loose-leaf binder in hand.

If sidewalks were trails, I might have seen and followed my old tracks leading to favorite haunts. But this time, as part of a master plan, I ventured well beyond previous routes to discover many new neighborhoods along the way. By journey's end, I discovered that a ritual of walking allows one to see the city from multiple perspectives as the streets and neighborhoods intertwine. Each block fits into a giant scheme that makes Lower Manhattan the best walking environment in the world.

BLoCkoLoGy (blŏk-ŏlə-jē) *n.*

1. The study of a city block's identity from one end to the other.

2. The close observation, while traveling on foot, of distinguishing urban characteristics, patterns, and themes. **Blockologist**: *n.* **1.** One who is an authority in blockology. **2.** An admirer of the urban scene.

WHAT IS A BLOCK?

An average dictionary will provide nearly 30 definitions for the word "block." You can find a "block" in an automobile, butcher's shop, auction house, stock market, playroom, and factory, while other varieties are located on train tracks, ships, and football fields, but hopefully not between your ears. "Block" also means to mold, support, press, hinder, forget, and prevent. Three distinct definitions for block pertain to a city. They are as follows: an apartment complex; the land confined by adjoining streets (as in Macy's sits *on a block*); and the meaning of choice for blockologists everywhere, a *segment of a street bounded by consecutive cross streets and including its buildings and inhabitants.*[2] This type of block is a whole world unto itself, a place where you might live, work, visit, and explore.

The character of a block is revealed in its details, through architectural styles, sidewalk and street surfaces, signs, posts, lights, hydrants, trees, plants, flowers, parks, playgrounds, fire escapes, gates, grates, vents, pipes, and storefront window displays. In Lower Manhattan, humanity from every corner of the globe frequents this segment of a city. While cars, trucks, buses, bicycles, and carts provide the mechanical seasoning for a block, pets provide an occasional seasoning of their own. This whole mélange is brought to you by a host of largely unknown architects, sign painters, window dressers, and community gardeners, who over decades and even centuries, have created blocks with distinct personalities just waiting to be discovered.

AN OBSERVATIONAL FEAST

No one who really sees Lower Manhattan leaves unaffected; it is an observational feast that can provide a lesson or two on what makes the city thrive. There is a block for every mood, sensibility, and interest. You get to know blocks that are meditative, active, utilitarian, historical, and modern. There are respected blocks and forgotten blocks. There are blocks with only restaurants and blocks with only shops, and blocks that offer just one cuisine, and some that simply sell shoes. There are blocks with wealthy people residing on one side of the street and poor on the other. And blocks with a single tree standing alone, while others are like parks. As you navigate your way through Lower Manhattan, there are choices to be made, toward the familiar or the unknown, with great urgency or at a slow pace. Endless bits of knowledge are filed away, vital information for future routes and future returns. You are the navigator of this pedmobile. Not only is there no direct way, there are unlimited possibilities for getting from here to there. This is where every urban admirer becomes a blockologist, adept at knowing blocks, their pluses and minuses and how they best connect. This allows you no small measure of control over your walking experience.

URBAN LITERACY

The vista on almost any street in Lower Manhattan is time recorded in the facades of buildings compressed side by side, subjected to incalculable alterations and reno-

2. "Block." *The Illustrated Heritage Dictionary and Information Book*. Boston: Houghton Mifflin Company, 1977: 142:13b.

HOW TO USE THIS BOOK

vations. There are many rows of townhouses or apartment buildings that were once identical that are now as different as they can be. Every decade's architectural preference since the 1820s is reflected in the facades of these blocks. How does one make sense of the multiplicity of styles, a never-ending meal of architectural tapas? To really walk Lower Manhattan, you must have reverence for the unexpected as a result of the city's passion for perpetual change. In addition, the proliferation of type on signs, clothing, and graffiti is enough to overwhelm the senses. How do you decide what to read, observe, or ignore?

The ability to make sense of visual chaos comes with time and observational osmosis, and it leads to urban literacy.

Blockology: An Offbeat Walking Guide to Lower Manhattan is for those who love exploring city blocks to make personal discoveries. With the help of easy-to-read maps, wander through the many neighborhoods of Lower Manhattan as you make your way to my own selection of 36 intriguing blocks. Each featured block comes with a detailed map, descriptive text, and a full-page illustration (a scavenger hunt of images). In addition, I've chosen plenty of "can't-miss blocks" which have been highlighted on the maps for your investigation along the way. So pick and choose and return again, until you experience all of Lower Manhattan for yourself. For the record, it took me 52 days and some 300 miles, moving as deliberately as possible, to walk every block below 14th Street.

Each featured illustration is created from a selection of my own photographs taken on that very street. The illustrations are intended to be an expressive archive of those selected blocks. Remember, all blocks in Lower Manhattan are transforming in some way, as renovation and development never cease. And when you add the constant turnover of restaurants and shops, the block you walk today will certainly be different when you return even a few seasons later.

The *Glossary*, in the rear of the book, defines characteristics, patterns, and themes found in the planned and unplanned urban landscape. Perhaps you will be able to add many that I have overlooked.* Draw your

* Send yours to blockology@turningcornerspress.com

own conclusions and share them with your companions. Try to assess what works and does not in some of the best walking neighborhoods in the world. Remember there is no shame in asking for directions. But with *Blockology* in hand, it is more likely that someone will ask them of you.

WEST VILLAGE & GREENWICH VILLAGE

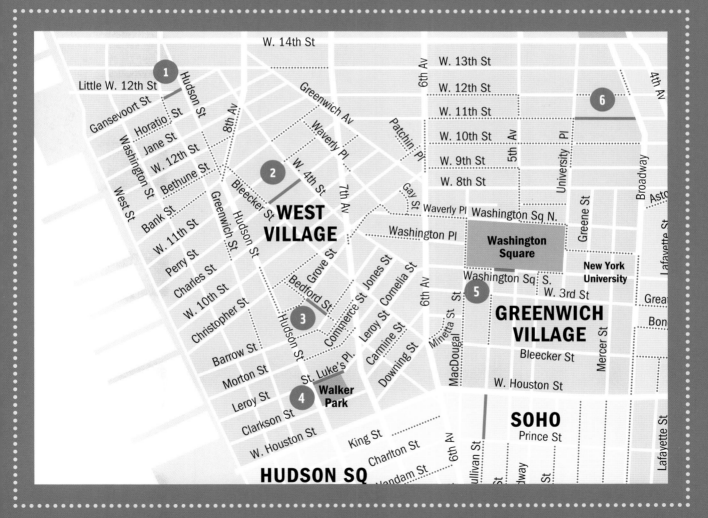

GANSEVOORT STREET GREENWICH & HUDSON STREETS

Multiple Perspectives

The wild crisscross of street patterns in Lower Manhattan created many triangularly shaped urban spaces. As city features go, right-angle intersection crossings cannot compare with triangles for sheer drama and romance. Gansevoort Street, with its multiple perspectives, perhaps has even influenced its residents to embrace radical points of view. And besides, to walk in the center of a triangular urban space is thrilling. It seems to elevate the importance of the individual.

Gustave Caillebotte, a late 18th century French painter, understood this truth and loved the spirit of wide-open urban panoramas. As an Impressionist painter, with a unique vision, he was enthralled with deep space, complex compositions, and the illusion of perspective. He painted a great number of canvases of Parisian sidewalks and cityscapes and would have felt right at home on this site on Gansevoort Street.[1]

The Meat Market District and its busy club scene has long been a destination for gays, transvestites, and high fashion models, who regularly cross paths with meatpacking workers in the wee hours. Residents, including artists and commercial proprietors, have for years occupied these spaces inexpensively due to the sight and smell of meat processing, the wild nightlife, and late-night truck deliveries. Those who loved both the chaotic mix and the architectural integrity fought successfully for the preservation of the recently declared Ganesvoort Market Historic District. Thankfully, this designation saves the architecture, but not necessarily the meat industry. Preservation often makes an area even more attractive and rapidly leads to the conversion of commercial property into residential.

The history of meat processing industry in New York City is one of frequent relocation from ever-encroaching residential populations. We are losing sight of the reason for cities in the first place. They were designed to be marketplaces of enormous variety that sustain multiple perspectives and serve the collective good.

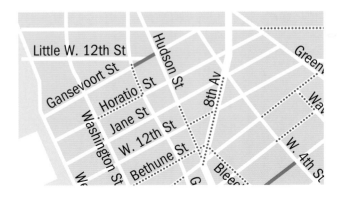

1. "Rue de Paris; Temps de Pluie" by Gustave Caillebotte, which may well be the world's most famous painting of an urban scene, is on display at The Art Institute of Chicago.

Planet Perry

Some blocks are nervous, while others are calm. No block in Lower Manhattan offers a more tranquil and graceful welcome than Perry Street between Bleecker and West 4th Streets. Some actually suspect that Perry is a park posing as a residential block, with its many planters and vines that hug the 19th century architecture. The sidewalk is double lined with mature trees that lean inward to form a luxuriant green canopy. Gated front gardens add yet an extra reason for these gardeners to plant. Such a striking landscape can only come with love and hard work, as observed by the liberally planted flowers within tree guards. This is, by the way, a group effort. "Plant it on Perry Street," the photocopied posters announce, along with the time and place for gardening neighbors to meet.

Elegant front stoops with ornate wrought iron railings abound on both sides of the street, with scalloped stairs that sweep up to grand entrances, such as #63, #64, #70, #74-76, and #80-82. There is a special unity to this block with a mix of brownstone and brick. A very old Federal Style structure at #85 was built in 1818. Since Lower Manhattan is an overwhelmingly rebuilt environment, it is always a novelty to discover an original structure that is as old as the block when it was first cut from farmland.

Renovation is ongoing as the block moves up to a new income bracket. Who wouldn't want to live on this block? It is interesting to note, however, that this neighborhood has always been too radical for both old money and the nouveau riche alike. Norman Mailer once resided at #73, Margaret Mead at #72[1] as well as the artist John Sloan at #61.[2] Here there is a long-established nonconformist spirit that is worth preserving as much as the architecture.

It is difficult to miss the most highly decorated and lushly landscaped basement hatch in all of Lower Manhattan on the corner of Bleecker Street. Above the elaborately embellished blue and white tile work, a wild bearded roman head proclaims Perry Street to be a world unto itself.

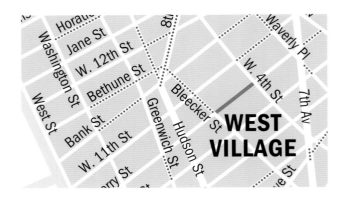

1. Naureckas, Jim. *New York Songlines: Perry Street*. 12 Sept. 2004 <http://www.nysonglines.com/>
2. Gaylord, Bruce Cranor. *Gaylord's Guides: The Only Complete Guide to Greenwich Village*. New York City: Gaylord Co., 1977: 93.

PERRY STREET

Text Block

This is a cloistered block, hard to find even for Lower Manhattanites. A quick overview of a map will explain why. This block is nestled within a small triangular area, wedged between three irregularly shaped neighborhoods, Hudson Square, the West Village and Greenwich Village. Consider the remote quality of this block, for it is surrounded by a multitude of busy streets, Bleecker, Christopher, Hudson, and Seventh Avenue South. Also notice how Seventh Avenue South cuts directly through this locale, slicing blocks at a 45 degree angle. The avenue came as a result of the construction of the IRT Subway line in 1914, and to this day, there is still evidence of the resulting odd buildings, and strange solutions on sharp plots of land.[1]

Outstanding Greek Revival architecture abounds among the trees, planters, and vines. With its many fine examples of varying sizes, shapes, and designs, Bedford Street should be known as the Museum of Exceptional Doors. The black garage doors at the J. Goebel & Co. building, and #85-

87, #88, and #84B are a few of the fine portals. The door at #86 is one you can actually enter and belongs to Chumley's, the popular but sign-less bar and restaurant. This former speakeasy has been a regular haunt for famous literati from the 1920s on, including John Dos Passos, Edna St. Vincent Millay, Theodore Dreiser,[2] Anais Nin, John Steinbeck, and Eugene O'Neill.[3] After you eat, you can leave using the other exit door on Barrow Street.

A walk in any season along Bedford and the bordering streets of Commerce, Morton, Leroy, and Carmine is the antidote to urban stress and over-stimulation. But for the authors who have lived here over the years it has meant so much more. Is there any doubt that these cloistered blocks offer the calm from which creative notions spring? Perhaps that is just what was intended all along in the original layout of the blocks, or more likely, the authors themselves fashioned it into the ideal setting for writing and reflection.

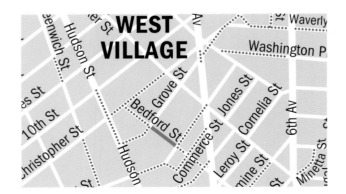

1. Gaylord, Bruce Cranor. *Gaylord's Guides: The Only Complete Guide to Greenwich Village.* New York City: Gaylord Co., 1977: 62.
2. Ibid.112
3. Naureckas, Jim. New York *Songlines: Bedford Street.* 31 Aug. 2004 <http://www.nysonglines.com/>

BEDFORD STREET

No Saint Jimmy

A stunning block of restored townhouses with ornately designed front stoops and figurative motifs hidden among the crawling vines and trees is laid open on the southern edge of the West Village. The equally impressive fence for James J. Walker Park aptly frames this short block and captures the spirit of old New York. One would never suspect what a peculiar place this has been.

One of the more surreal visions in all of Lower Manhattan is encountered here. Stand by the park near the Public Library facing west. Allow your right eye to capture the row of townhouses, while your left eye embraces Keith Haring's long mural by the swimming pool. This cherished recreational park is the only one of its kind for miles and has been through many park configurations. It began as St. John's Cemetery, then transformed into St. John's Park, followed by Hudson Park to its present incarnation as a baseball field.

For nearly a century, this block has been under the spell of Mayor Jimmy Walker. That provocative leader grew up here as child and continued to live at #6 with his wife and family for many years. The mayor, also known as "Beau James," presided over New York City during the Roaring Twenties as the unabashed symbol of the new modern male, fashionable, free spirited and unaffected by the restrictive mores of the past. He just went a little too far. In one of the strangest episodes in New York City history, Mayor Walker had the name of this block changed from Leroy Street, (or at least 3/4 of it) to St. Luke's Place. His dubious goal was to obscure his mistress' address, which happened to be right at the east end of the block.[1] He eventually had to resign because of a bribery scandal and his extra marital affair.

The divorced ex-mayor would marry his mistress, Betty Compton, and take up residence on East 72nd Street on a block far more in keeping with his Swing Era sensibilities.[2] How ironic that James J. Walker's legacy is "forever" secured, fenced in, on the very block that had confined him, for better or for worse, for so many years. "Beau James" would have much preferred an uptown address.

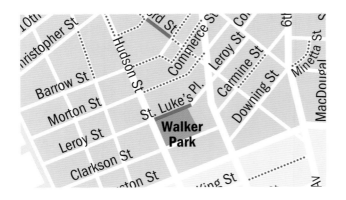

1. Harris, Bill, Photographs by Jorg Brockmann. *One Thousand New York Buildings*, New York: Black Dog and Leventhal Publishers, 2002: 146.
2. Fowler, Gene, "Walker, James J." *The Encyclopedia of New York City*. New Haven: Yale University Press, 1995.

ST. LUKE'S PLACE

Square, Park, or Quad?

Washington Place South is the main concourse for the campus of New York University. NYU set up shop in 1837 on the northeastern edge of this turbulent piece of ground that was once a cemetery holding over 10,000 bodies. It was also a popular destination for dueling and public executions.[1] Even though NYU owns most of the property surrounding Washington Square Park, it was never able to establish a unified vision or anything close to an ideal of a campus quadrangle insulated from the harsh realities of life. On the contrary, free-thinking artists and bohemians have long dominated the spirit of this place. Although once a year NYU takes over Washington Square Park for a graduation ceremony, the park's character and that of the University seem to be eternally at cross-purposes. Ironically, the park is a great recruiter of students for NYU.

Washington Place South has only three buildings, all moving in radically different directions. The Italian Renaissance American Baptist Judson Memorial Church with its soaring bell tower is an NYU acquisition, but could not have been a better choice as the centerpiece for a quadrangle campus had the school planned for it. The Stanford White design is otherworldly, as if purchased by J.P. Morgan and moved here brick by brick from some Italian hill town. All that is missing to complete the fantasy is a Chianti vineyard across the street.

The Skirball Department of Hebrew and Judaic Studies and the Hapgop Kervorkian Center of Middle Eastern Studies, designed by Phillip Johnson and Richard Foster, complete the block. If one cannot design for continuity, then you might as well celebrate contrasts. Regardless of the success or failure of this arrangement, NYU created perhaps accidentally a block that symbolizes three great cultures and religions sharing common walls, an ideal easily embraced by Lower Manhattan.

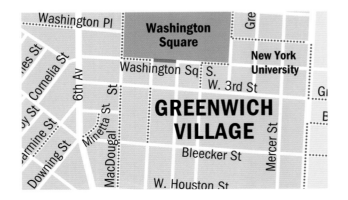

1. Wolfe, Gerard R. *New York, A Guide to the Metropolis.* New York: McGraw Hill, 1988: 89

WASHINGTON PLACE SOUTH

Warhol's Haunt

The artist and shopper extraordinaire, Andy Warhol, spent many exhilarated days on this block. Here you will find more than a dozen antique stores in a classic environment that puts the buyer in just the right mood. Blocks that sell a single type of merchandise are common in Lower Manhattan, whether it is shoes, lamps, stoves, or antiques. These item blocks cannot help but assume the persona of their goods, and besides they offer great convenience, competition, and character. Retail districts still develop spontaneously in Lower Manhattan for a public that rewards every marketable idea and considers shopping as a high art.

If you watch PBS's Antiques Road Show, then you already know never, ever to refinish an 18th century side table. It destroys the integrity of the piece and decreases the resale value tenfold. If buildings were like furniture, the cast-iron gem at #67, once known for McCreery's Dry Goods and an early version of a department store, would have been preserved intact, rather than suffer the 1971 penthouse addition that increased its size.[1] Even today these mod-tops continue to proliferate. Stylistic contrast is the hallmark of Lower Manhattan, but to force two styles into a single building creates architectural absurdities and disrupts the continuity of a block.

The Gothic-influenced Grace Church on Broadway, designed by James Renwick Jr., sits on a unique site where Broadway bends. This slight turn affords remarkable views and adds a bit of intrigue to a city organized in straight lines. When an entire block such as East 11th Street is devoted to one mode of retail, adjoining blocks must provide variety and everyday essential services. University Place does just that with grocery stores, dry cleaners, pharmacies, restaurants, and superb coffee shops. There, one can contemplate the price and merit of a Louis XIV vase over a cheeseburger and fries.

1. White, Norval, Elliot Willensky, *AIA Guide to New York City*. New York: Three Rivers Press, 2000: 165

NOHO & EAST VILLAGE

A Stable Environment

Three parking lots would kill most blocks, but Great Jones somehow maintains its dignity. The landmark Engine Co. #33, along with the open framework parking elevators that mimic the skeletal understructure of its neighboring cast-iron buildings, dominates this block of parking lots. Even the fire escapes get into the act, visually unifying the block with complicated latticework patterns reaching high up into the sky. This block was built to take a beating, with granite sidewalks and iron loading docks. It survives as an eclectic mix of automobile and old-fashioned commercial intentions.

Great Jones abounds in buildings with decorative motifs that offer the contrast of elegance in the face of fulfilling everyday service needs. The Greek Revival commercial structures with their "drawings in stone" of patterns, shells, palm leaves, lion heads, and flowers are constant reminders of an era that encouraged grace and craftsmanship for public display, not merely for the isolated rich. And how many blocks can claim unique utilitarian sculptures such as the rocketshipesque configuration on the northwest sidewalk and the jet engine fan protruding from the Great Jones Café near Bowery?

The cornices at #31 and #33 speak proudly of a prior era devoted to the horse. Even though autos have long replaced the four-legged creatures, compartmentalization remains the central guiding principle with "stables" for horsepower—cars perched high above the sidewalk patiently await their master's return. The large open spaces of parking lots add the unintended benefit of revealing outstanding 19th century architecture on West 4th and Lafayette Street, along with vast weathered expanses of brick walls. On most days light saturates this block, seemingly from all angles. But to truly appreciate Great Jones, it must be seen in the fog in endless shades of gray, as it calls forth memories of an older working class city.

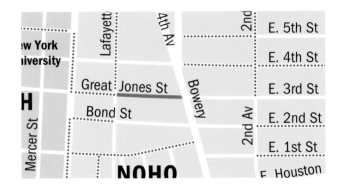

GREAT JONES STREET

Sea of Contrasts

On any summer night, one can watch people pour out of the Second Avenue Subway Station at Houston Street and First Avenue. There is a sense of arrival in the air. Most folks make a left turn and head north past the local landmark—the neon Gringer Appliance sign. This portal block acts as a southern entrance to the East Village, and there might as well be a triumphant arch spanning this expansive avenue. For the neighborhood, the local stores satisfy every basic need, but there is broader appeal here as a destination for the popular restaurants, clubs, and specialty shops, such as Boca Chica, Lucien, Lucky Chengs, and Tattoo.

Hispanic culture has resided in this neighborhood since the 1950s, and it blends with a myriad of others, including the Sikh taxi drivers who take their breaks on East Houston Street. Meanwhile, memorial services at the Ortiz Funeral Home spill out onto the sidewalk. Pedestrians somehow intertwine with grieving attendees without breaking stride or interrupting the flow of conversation.

First Avenue is a thoroughfare for automobiles, even though the timing of the lights does not permit racing. Five full lanes are a long way for a person to cross, but the dark trees with broad roots manage it easily with their long branches suspended far over the avenue. Likewise, these broad trees strikingly frame the old tenements and wildly colorful storefronts.

This block hosts a candidate for the most creative mod-top for a tenement building in Lower Manhattan. Observe on the southwest corner a traditional New England style widow's watch high above the street, which at first glance is totally out of character with the surrounding architecture. What an odd, but fitting arrangement, looking down over a sea of contrasts onto a remarkable block that is both lively and intimate, free-spirited yet rooted in tradition.

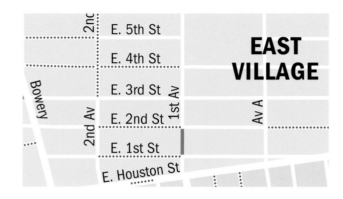

FIRST AVENUE

Underlying Character

One of the great attributes of a block in Lower Manhattan is how the past lives on not just in its buildings and businesses, but also in its underlying character. A sense of play is the theme that has survived through the likes of the Orpheum Theater and retail shops such as Wows!ville, Toy Tokyo, Love Saves the Day, and Tiger, Titus and Toes.

The Orpheum Theater is a relic of the era when Second Avenue was known as the Jewish Rialto and was home to the Yiddish Theater. Is it possible that even though a whole form of entertainment nearly vanished from the scene, its undying spirit simply reshaped itself to reach a new audience? New Yorkers count on their blocks, and performing old habits die-hard. The theater spectacle has simply moved out on to the street. The sidewalks are 21-feet-wide and can accommodate a huge flow of foot traffic, which moves at a 2nd Avenue amble rather than a Broadway stride. On this rally block there is much to take in: the seated customers at The Visage outdoor café, the old fashioned B&H sign, and the lively conversations in front of The Ukrainian Sport Club.

This block becomes even more intriguing when you notice that it is sandwiched between two elite, erudite institutions: NYU to the south and to the north the landmark Ottendorfer Branch of the New York Public Library that once defined this old German community. Is there meaning in this close proximity of radically different purposes? Lower Manhattan has always celebrated life compressed—the closer, the better in all things, activities, and people.[1]

For those who know this block well, and return time and again to promenade much the way that people did generations ago, they draw endless satisfaction from the free activity of walking in the city. It is not Second Avenue alone that sustains this thrill, but the many great blocks that lie just around the corner and throughout the East Village.

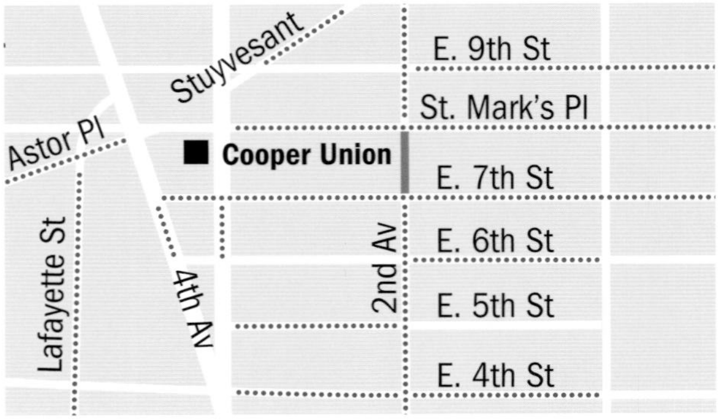

[Map showing streets: Astor Pl, Stuyvesant, Lafayette St, 4th Av, 2nd Av, Cooper Union, E. 9th St, St. Mark's Pl, E. 7th St, E. 6th St, E. 5th St, E. 4th St]

[1]. An elevated transit line once occupied Second Avenue, but now it is slated for a new subway line that has caused great concern in this neighborhood. If it arrives on schedule, it will be here in 2016.

SECOND AVENUE

Gathering Notions

East 10th Street is a revitalized block with a public library, café, bakery, restaurant, and attractive residences. It is also on the edge of Tompkins Square Park. At present, no other park in the city is used better or valued more. But what a wild ride it has been to reach this favorable point.

The Commissioner's Plan of 1811 was the first real attempt at urban planning for the City of New York. The original design for this site included a long park extending all the way to the East River. What a novel idea to bring the waterfront into the city, and open up views of the river. But it never happened. An alternative, seemingly benign plan was implemented in 1834,[1] with the creation of a dignified park surrounded by well-to-do residential blocks. Shortly thereafter, German immigrants densely populated this area known as Kleindeutchland, Little Germany, or Dutchtown (a misuse of the word Deutsche).[2] These urbane newcomers brought with them socialist ideals that included the notion of strength-in-numbers, and they used Tompkins Square as a gathering place for political protests. After the bread riots and draft riots, this spot ceased being a park and became a national guard parade ground. The park was back for a second chance in 1879,[3] and again the residents' rousing appeals for social reform and the labor movement filled the block and resonated off the surrounding buildings.

The German community later relocated to Yorkville on the Upper East Side, but Tompkins Square would maintain its contentious reputation far into the next century, as the neighborhood became a center for alternative lifestyles. Ultimately, the homeless overwhelmed the park, which led in 1988 to a violent and controversial struggle with the police. Add to the mix, drug addicts and their dealers, and Tompkins Square Park closed for renovations in 1991.[4]

The park reopened with a curfew that made for a more welcoming square for children and their parents, and dogs and their owners, without discouraging nonconformist views. It is curious how things do not quite work out as planned, but then eventually turn out for the better. No one person could have thought up this place, an egalitarian block with a park where many gather and freely express all sorts of notions.

1. Burrows, Edwin G., Mike Wallace, *Gotham: A History of New York City to 1898.* New York: Oxford University Press, 1999: 579
2. Sanders, Ronald, photographs by Edmund V. Gillon, Jr. *The Lower East Side: A Guide to Its Jewish Past in 99 New Photographs.* New York: Dover Publications, 1994:19
3. Naureckas, Jim. *New York Songlines: 10th Street.* 12 Sept. 2004 <http://www.nysonglines.com/>
4. Mipaas, Esther. "Tompkins Square." *The Encyclopedia of New York City,* New Haven: Yale University Press, 1995.

EAST 10TH STREET

AVENUE C   EAST 8TH & 9TH STREETS

Where Nature Survives

Some blocks thrive through great luck, a blessed location, or wealth that buys elegance and protection. Avenue C is about people, at their best and worst, and perseverance through unbelievable adversity. This is the block to go when world events seem overwhelming, where a chain-link fence is a symbol of commitment and creativity, not indifference, and a bench is to sit on, not to sleep. Avenue C is an unusual yet harmonious mix of influences, where each tells an important story.

Not that long ago, this was a dangerous neighborhood of drug addicts and dealers. The park on the northwest corner embodies the revival of a community by residents who never lost hope. That hope came from the 600 B/C East 9th Street Block Association that took a large vacant lot in 1976 and converted it into La Plaza Cultural Park. Less than thirty years later, the mature willows express a majesty that takes your breath away. It is a miracle that the park is still here, as the city had plans to build upon this site in 1986 that were successfully defeated by La Plaza Defense League.[1] That would be the first of many legal battles to come.

Over the last 30 years, Community or Green Thumb Gardens sprang up all over the East Village turning hellish vacant lots miraculously into pocket parks. Each one has a character all its own due to this diverse volunteerism. During Mayor Guiliani's administration, an attempt was made to auction off many of the Green Thumbs. It would take a lawsuit from the State of New York against the city to put an end to this threatened action.[2] And in a recent decision, The NYC Community Gardens Agreement, both La Plaza Cultural Park and the 9th Street Community Garden on Avenue C will receive permanent preservation status through either the Parks Department or a nonprofit land trust.

A truly relaxed spirit thrives on this block along Avenue C, which belies its history of once-overcrowded tenements, drug wars, and community-action legal battles. The mix of restaurants, cafes, an art-inspired vacant lot, the stunning view of the parks and even the new architecturally engaging Public Service Administration Building #4 create an atmosphere of harmony. A perfect place to learn from where nature survives.

Map showing Tompkins Square, Av A, Av B, Av C, Szold Pl, Av D, and E. 7th St through E. 12th St.

1. *La Plaza Cultural; an East Village Oasis.* 17 Aug. 2004 http://www.laplazacultural.org/history.html
2. Bill Not Bored. *Community Gardens in New York City: the Lower East Side of Manhattan.* 17 Aug. 2004 <http://www.notbored.org/gardens.html>

AVENUE C

LOWER EAST SIDE

Dos Floristas

The foliage on this block of Clinton Street beckons, especially on a hot day, since it must be at least twenty degrees cooler in the shade. This easy-going block was once a haven for drug addicts, but now has become a popular destination for nightlife. This is the story of a block that went from one extreme to the other.

Economic distress has been a century old condition in this quarter of the Lower East Side; nonetheless it has had a succession of tight-knit communities. In what was once a Jewish neighborhood, Congregation Chasam Sopher is a reminder of those days past. This place of worship has a long legacy, dating back to 1891,[1] and has continued to remain open even when the neighborhood became predominately Hispanic. The 70s and 80s were filled with drugs and violence, but over the last decade this block has become safer, cleaner, and more beautiful, in large measure thanks to the many long-term residents and predominately Latino-owned businesses. In recent years, Clinton Street slowly transitioned into a block with a wider assortment of stores, clientele and cultural backgrounds, who were no less dedicated. It flourished as a crossroads block with equal parts of ethnic character and contemporary trends. In this distinct natural setting, that unique mix drew crowds.

Clinton Street soon became identified as a hot block, and the landlords rushed to cash in. The renovations began. In a flash, by spring of 2004, a large number of Latino businesses closed down or moved out, including two florists on opposite sides of the block. Irony never ends in Lower Manhattan. Clinton Street became popular, because of the dynamic cultural mix, but now it has little. That is cold comfort for those who invested themselves and saw its potential.

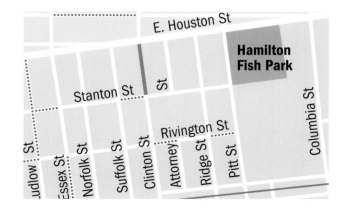

1. Sanders, Ronald, photographs by Edmund V. Gillon, Jr. *The Lower East Side: A Guide to Its Jewish Past in 99 New Photographs.* New York: Dover Publications, 1994: 36

CLINTON STREET

ORCHARD STREET DELANCEY & RIVINGTON STREETS

Sales Pitch

This is a tag block from as far back as anyone can remember. Clothing is sold in almost every storefront, with hanging coats, shirts, and dresses suspended from awning metalwork above the sidewalk. Hats, shoes, gloves, underwear, and socks are all displayed on tables, as salesmen hawk their wares and loudly converse with their counterparts across the street. The old signs blend with the new like wallpaper in a cheap motel. The S. Berkenstein sign painted on #130 is alone worth a visit to New York City. With rows of tenement apartment buildings and the discount retail establishments, it does not take much imagination to see old Lower East Side life with pushcarts and masses of humanity roaming about. This antique image defines New York City and is held dear in the hearts of the descendants of the many immigrants who once settled here.

Yet New York has never been a place that has held on to the past to delay the future. This can be a cruel realization for those who love a certain corner or block. The city that tore down George Washington's home and Penn Station is not restrained by sentiment.

Thankfully, preservationists have made strides since then, protecting areas like Greenwich Village, SoHo, TriBeCa, and recently Ganesvoort Market. Developers seem to believe that our heritage must be razed on a daily basis or we will all end up forever trapped in the past.

But how long will Orchard remain as it is? It still retains its old-world character through its architecture and the art of the sales pitch, a tradition as old as the first cities. The next block to the south on Orchard is the home of the Lower East Side Tenement Museum that attracts visitors from all over the world, eager to get a clear glimpse into past of what the Lower East Side was once like. But on the block to the north, you will encounter the East Village atmosphere with restaurants, clubs, cafes, and specialty shops that have moved in recently. It is a block that would certainly shock, but equally intrigue our ancestors, if they could see all the new items for sale displayed in an old yet familiar package.

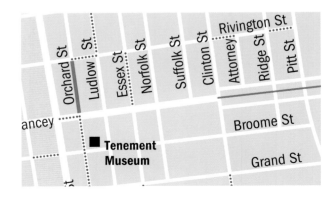

ORCHARD STREET

Returning Once Again

Here the land slopes gently down to the East River, where once stunning river views, farmland, and easy access to water transportation attracted the well-to-do Dutch settlers in the 1700s. As the next century unfolded, shipbuilding grew and established itself, and a merchant class occupied the area.[1] By the 1880s, Henry Street and the Seventh Ward had become a neighborhood thick with tenements for low-income housing serving the needs of the recent Jewish immigrants. Population density and living conditions were extremely poor to miserable, but never did the wave of immigration cease. The city did little to assist in the assimilation, so private humanitarian agencies stepped in. Of crucial importance was the Henry Street Settlement, founded by Lillian Ward in 1895 and funded by the philanthropist Jacob Schiff. The Settlement provided nursing care, health education, and a revolutionary range of social services that went way beyond the norm and included recreation, arts, and culture.

Henry Street today is a strange, but moving, vision of the history of the Lower East Side stretched out on one long block, offering a wide spectrum from dilapidated structures to public housing to pristine landmarks. The Greek Revival townhouses at #263, #265, and #267 would not likely be here if not for The Settlement's occupancy and long commitment to the area. The firehouse of Engine Co. #15 and one of the older churches in Manhattan, St. Augustine's Chapel from 1828, are also preserved. The 1930s would bring a new vision for Henry Street with the construction of public housing—the Vladek Houses. In the 1950s, The Henrietta Szold School (PS 134) was added, along with the Sol Lain Playground.

The block may deteriorate toward Grand Street, but somehow all the open space and variety of architecture is held together by mature oak trees and cobblestone edging on the sidewalks. In large measure because of the extensive planting among the public housing throughout the area, the landscape is returning once again.

1. Burrows, Edwin G., Mike Wallace, *Gotham: A History of New York City to 1898*. New York: Oxford University Press, 1999: 340

HENRY STREET

ESSEX STREET CANAL & HESTER STREETS

Change is a Constant

From the early Dutch settlement on, Lower Manhattan has had very few parks. Residential and commercial needs have always taken precedent. The vast majority of present day parks were once cemeteries or the result of slum clearance projects, especially in the Lower East Side. In the 1890s this location was considered to be the one of the most densely populated areas in human history. William H. Seward Park across from Essex Street, named after Lincoln's Secretary of State, was created in 1900 as an attempt to lessen overcrowding, while providing the healthful benefits of green space and fresh air. And in an inspired vision, a Carnegie Free Public Library was added shortly thereafter on the east-end of the park. Interestingly, the park once extended farther north until public housing was built there some 30 years later.[1] In the eyes of city planners there were first too many people, then not enough, or not enough parkland, then too much. In any event, even though many of the original tenement buildings are intact, change is a constant here.

This is a seminal site, once the heart and soul of the Jewish community. Just southeast at 175 East Broadway, stands the Forward Building, home of the influential Yiddish newspaper, the Jewish Daily Forward. It is now a block undergoing yet more change as the Asian community begins to invest in the storefronts on Essex, supplanting the Jewish-run businesses. This is a crossroads community now with the blending of Hispanic, Chinese, and Jewish cultures. Each has its own shops, restaurants, and institutions, best seen in the activity at the intersection of Essex and Canal at Nathan Straus Square, named for the great philanthropist and co-owner of R.H. Macy's.

Essex Street itself has a mix of stores ranging from the Main Squeeze, an accordion shop, to Israeli imports. The Chinese and Hebrew signs create a collage of symbols, with an occasional English translation. The M. Schames Paint Store with its prominent sign anchors the block and recalls earlier days, while the modern white high-rise several doors down provides outstanding park views for its residents, views that will certainly also change.

1. Sanders, Ronald, photographs by Edmund V. Gillon, Jr. *The Lower East Side: A Guide to Its Jewish Past in 99 New Photographs.* New York: Dover Publications, 1994: 53

ESSEX STREET

LITTLE ITALY, NOLITA, & THE BOWERY

Alfresco

There are many neighborhoods that define Lower Manhattan, yet none is more seductive than Little Italy. As a tight-knit Italian American community, it has long captivated the city for its big shots and local character in specialty food shops, social clubs, and restaurants. The image of this neighborhood includes major doses of Mafia-inspired icons, fueled recently by HBO's *The Sopranos,* and a long ago, but not forgotten mob hit of Joey Gallo, all of which adds an element of imagined peril when ordering scungilli.[1] In reality, organized crime pervaded all ethnic groups and neighborhoods, including even Wall Street. For that matter, mob hits occurred throughout the city, wherever the opportunity presented itself. At some point, this stereotyped and cinematically inspired portrait needs to die. That is perhaps easier said than done in a city forever steeped in mythic history.

Now the city is faced with a shrinking Italian community within Little Italy. What exists is still vital; however, it is so much smaller than a decade ago. Most New Yorkers would be heartsick at the thought of its disappearance, but the transition of ethnic neighborhoods has always been a cruel fact of life in Lower Manhattan. We can preserve buildings, but not culture, and attempts to do so become canned and artificial.

Most neighborhoods have blocks of many intentions, including shopping, essential services, and residential. Little Italy is losing those blocks in favor of menu blocks. Mulberry Street is a block for restaurants that provides a lively New York experience, a place to dine well in a festive alfresco atmosphere with a view of the Empire State.

The most diverse walking adventure you can possibly have in all of Lower Manhattan is to travel one block east to Mott Street on the same cross streets. There you will encounter a sensationally authentic market block that is completely within the Asian community—a part of Chinatown expanding into Little Italy. This walk describes what is truly remarkable about a delightfully diverse Lower Manhattan, but brings to the surface a longing for an old neighborhood with an uncertain future.

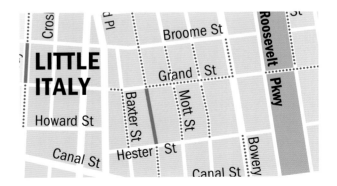

1. Tuohy, John William, Ed Becker, "Umberto's Clam House Opens for Business and Bullets, Again." Rick Porrello's American Mafia.com, 12 Sept. 2004 <http://www.amercanmafia.com/Feature_Articles_46.html>

MULBERRY STREET

Indoors and Out

Intimate Elizabeth Street caters to hoards of fashion conscious shoppers who seek a blouse, a belt, or a pair of shoes. This promenade of boutiques is packed into storefronts end to end and topped by stunning residential architecture. These ultra stylish shops arrived as a reasonable alternative to high-rent SoHo and found a niche in a popular retail district called NoLita (North of Little Italy). Even though boutiques dominate Elizabeth Street, the underlying ethnic spirit is seen in the occasional storefronts, butcher shops, and the public displays of national heritage on fire escapes.

The pace in the morning can be slow, so slow that employees stand or squat in front of their storefronts talking on cell phones or smoking cigarettes. It certainly gets busy, though, as the afternoon progresses. A dedicated shopper could spend an entire day on this block, by either walking south to Café Habana or north to Café Colonial. And if one should tire in between, there are benches to sit on both in front of stores and around trees. Not long ago in Lower Manhattan, a sidewalk bench was nearly impossible to find. This particular area of East Houston Street and Bowery had a long reputation as a gathering spot for homeless men, but in recent years their numbers have dwindled to the point that an employee from a local shelter expressed his concern to me about losing his job.

Elizabeth Street may be lined with shops, but it is a far different experience than a stroll through a climate-controlled windowless corridor. Here shoppers actually interact with the elements, not only in fair weather, but also on days of sweltering heat and freezing cold. For those who love shopping, nothing compares to the rush of excitement upon entering a new store. But for those who love sidewalks, a view from the nearest bench is the best spot to watch the shoppers wander indoors and out.

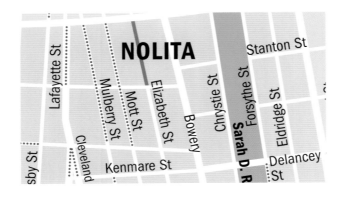

ELIZABETH STREET

Teenage Heaven

What street is more appropriately named than Broadway? Once a Native American Lenape trail, it is the trunk of the tree that grew Manhattan. It extends seventeen miles up Manhattan Island and then all the way to Albany and a bit beyond.[1]

For teenagers throughout the New York metropolitan area, Broadway is *the* place to shop. It is a rite of passage for suburban teens to explore New York City with their shopping buddies. They enter by commuter train into a world that is beyond belief, where choice seems infinite, and fascinating blocks lead in all directions. Broadway at Grand Street only intensifies that experience with a tag block solely devoted to the latest teenage craze in fashion and accessories. In spite of the "mall-ing" of the entire metropolitan area, the density and excitement of shopping in Manhattan has never been duplicated. Any suburban teenager will confirm this. So they come in waves to shop at Yellow Rat Bastard, Necessary Clothing, O.M.G., and Alice Underground. It slays any suburban shopping adventure.

What goes around, comes around, for this block was once the heart of a very fash-ionable shopping district in the mid-nineteenth century with Lord and Taylor's at this intersection.[2] The art of shopping would evolve into a preference for department stores, such as the very first ones—A.T. Stewart's, R.H. Macy's, and Wanamaker's. They were housed further up Broadway near Union Square, and by the 1880s, many more flourished along Broadway and Sixth Avenue toward 23rd Street. This was known as Ladies' Mile, but as the decades rolled by these stores moved even farther away from Lower Manhattan.

Bloomingdale's has long been a midtown department store at 59th Street between Lexington and Third Avenue. With great fanfare, a satellite store recently opened downtown on Broadway, above Broome Street at the former site of Canal Jeans. Will other department stores follow? Does this mean the end of the independent stores on this ribbon of Broadway? Most likely, but free-spirited stores such as these are destined to spring up elsewhere once again creating the latest hot shopping block. This rite of passage cannot be denied.

1. Elsroad, Linda. "Broadway." *The Encyclopedia of New York City*. New Haven: Yale University Press, 1995.
2. Trager, James. *The New York Chronology*. New York: Harper Collins, 2003:141

BROADWAY

SOHO &
HUDSON SQUARE

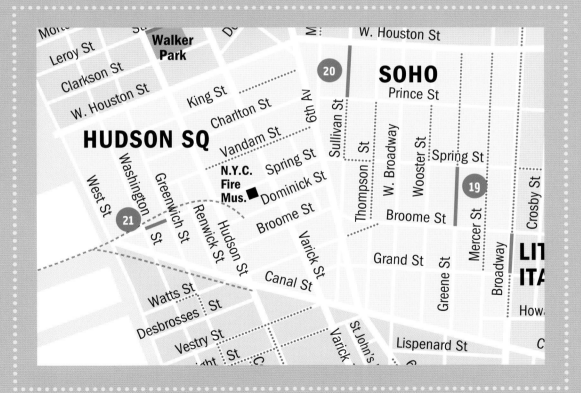

A Different Kind of Noise

Furniture and antique shops predominate on this block, with Nuovo, Modernica, Boca Grande, British Khaki, and Greene Street Antiques. These stores tend to attract buyers with deep pockets. Greene Street in all its cast-iron glory most decidedly runs at a slower pace than Spring Street to the north, which is crowded with tourists, shoppers, and a steady stream of sightseeing buses.

Most of the artists who revitalized this neighborhood of SoHo are gone, long replaced by residents with a higher standard of living. Rents, both for commercial and residential property, are through the roof, destabilizing a neighborhood that has become a victim of its own success. But as far as the passerby is concerned, this block could not be more attractive with its elegant white cast-iron architecture, loading docks with metal steps, and a cobblestone street that defines the district. Cobblestone paving is still prevalent in Lower Manhattan and adds a touch of old world charm, especially when it rains. But those cobblestones pro-

duce a bone-rattling noise from trucks as they race up the block.

Just thirty years ago, it was another world here. Huge semi trucks would back straight up to the loading docks, blocking the entire street. This was true for chic West Broadway as well. It would take a pedestrian twice the time to negotiate around these trucks in a chaotic scene of movers and foremen. A different kind of noise prevailed then, the raucous sound of the street. Then the area quickly transitioned as the dark, soot-covered buildings provided great opportunities for gigantic galleries and later for stores. Another change waits on the horizon, and it seems benign enough. Trees are being planted in greater numbers throughout this firmly established residential neighborhood. With a greener Greene Street coming soon, the original, working-class character of this neighborhood will be impossible to picture. How can a historically preserved district feel so different with each passing decade?

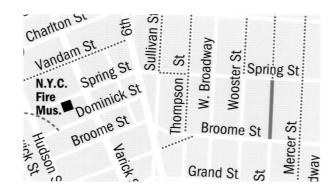

GREENE STREET

The Slice of Life

On any Lower Manhattan map, Sullivan Street is listed as a part of SoHo, but it actually lies on the edge of that historic cast-iron district, well within its own close-knit community comprised of MacDougal, Thompson, Spring, and Prince streets, bordered by Canal and West Houston. These few blocks are lined with traditional style tenements and an occasional Greek Revival townhouse, and have a special character of their own. The Greenwich Village Society for Historic Preservation has set up a campaign to preserve these blocks within an area called the South Village that reaches up to Washington Square Park.[1]

West Houston Street to the north moves huge numbers of cars, trucks and pedestrians along an east-west length that crosses Manhattan Island. But just imagine if the Dutch had prevailed in ruling New Amsterdam instead of the British, then Houston Street would certainly be a canal, a waterway with crossing bridges extending as far as the eye could see with bicycles criss-crossing everywhere.

But that was not to be as other cultures also left their mark on Lower Manhattan, especially the Italians on Sullivan Street. Their influence is pervasive with the distinctive presence of St. Anthony of Padua Church and the figurative sculptures of Mary and St. Anthony himself. Churches are centers for gathering all during the week; a long tradition exists for residents to stand and converse on this end of the block with the Empire State Building as a backdrop.

A lifestyle where food, family and church are fundamental is all encompassing here. Joe's Dairy, Pino's Meats, and Pepe Rosso to Go are the mainstays on the street and have excellent and well-deserved reputations. A California friend of mine, when on business in New York, makes a pilgrimage to Joe's. He patiently waits in line savoring the atmosphere, then purchases several pounds of freshly braided, wet mozzarella along with the smoked variety to bring back to his family, who eagerly await his arrival and divide up the treats before his suitcase hits the floor. They know of what they taste—thick slices of Sullivan Street.

1. *Protecting the South Village.* The Greenwich Village Society for Historic Preservation. 18 Aug. 2004 <http://www.gvshp.org/southvillage.htm>

SULLIVAN STREET

21

Comings and Goings

You may not be aware that you are standing high above the western extension of the Holland Tunnel. The huge ventilation structure just past Washington Street is a testament to the tunnel's unseen presence, with a second rising from Pier 34 farther in the distance. Since 1927, millions of trucks, buses, and automobiles have passed under Spring Street, headed for New Jersey and points west. At one time or another, probably every town across the country has been as a destination.

The Hudson River used to kiss the shore here back before landfill extended Manhattan Island another block west beyond Washington Street. The iron bollard by the Ear Inn is a fitting reminder of those colonial days when ships once anchored here and arrived from and departed for ports throughout the world. The piers fell into disuse and decline by the 1950s, but that legacy also helped shape this block.

The Ear Inn, its name derived from a neon sign mutation, has had a long and colorful history since 1817 as a brewery,

brothel, speakeasy, bar, and restaurant, and is a favorite spot for local residents and laborers. In Lower Manhattan where so many shops and restaurants come and go, the steady presence of an unpretentious institution like the Ear Inn is held dear.

On the north side of Spring Street sits the stylish, but somewhat neglected United Parcel Service Building. At four stories tall, it may appear unassuming, yet this giant shipping depot fills the entire length of two long blocks. No one would know from this vantage-point, that all the delivery trucks come and go on Greenwich and Washington Streets. Unfortunately, the sleek main entrance to the UPS building is no longer in use as employees enter on West Houston Street or through side entrances. A new restaurant, Tres Truffles, is an upscale indication of the changing character of this Hudson Square neighborhood, and now occupies the UPS storefront. It only has a couple of hundred years to go to catch up to the Ear Inn.

1. Major development is a real possibility for Spring Street, both next to the Ear Inn and on the enormous parking lot between Washington and West Streets.

SPRING STREET

TRIBECA

22

ERICSSON PLACE HUDSON & VARICK STREETS

In All Directions

During the 1890s, horse-drawn lorries lined up on this cobblestone street devoted to manufacturing ice blocks. Known as Beach Street on beautiful Hudson Square, it was renamed in honor of John Ericsson, the Swedish born mechanical engineer and inventor of the ironclad Civil War ship, the Monitor, who resided on this block at #36 for many years.[1]

Ericsson Place is best recognized for the NYPD's 1st Precinct Station on the corner of Varick Street, seen again and again in background shots for film and television. Its elegantly rugged appearance best illustrates the character of the Police Department and the working class spirit that still remains in the facades of many of the street's buildings and loading docks.

Ericsson Place is on the southern end the Holland Tunnel Auto Exit Plaza that disperses cars in all directions. It is quite a feat as nine lanes at the New Jersey side tollgate must merge to two. Space is so precious in Lower Manhattan that it cannot allow for a huge cloverleaf to accomplish this task. Here cars, lots of them—16,566,000 a year[2]—must coexist with an awful lot of people. The Port Authority of NY & NJ recently completed a rehabilitation of the Exit Plaza to try to address this issue. You be the judge.

Is this the American version of a European square, only in this case for a citizenry on wheels? Blockologists need to look up and around at the architectural grandeur of the four blocks, especially on Ericsson, Hudson, and Laight. A walk over the pedestrian bridge on the northern end of the plaza allows one to observe the entire expanse of this site and ponder the sheer volume of activity.

Most street names in Lower Manhattan have little relationship with their contemporary look or significance. Not so for this place. The engineering genius of the Holland Tunnel and the steady stream of automobiles would have enthralled John Ericsson. For the rest of us, watch where you cross.

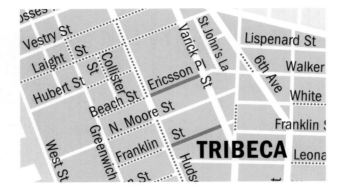

1. Moscow, Henry. *The Street Book: An Encyclopedia of Manhattan's Street Names and Their Origins,* New York: Fordham University Press, 1978: 48

2. Holland Tunnel Statistics: 2003. *The Port Authority of NY& NJ.* 31 Aug. 2004
<http://www.panynj.gov/tbt/htframe.HTM>

ERICSSON STREET

Romanesque Revival Meeting

TriBeCa, once referred to as the Lower West Side, was rebuilt with warehouses in the late 1800s to serve a burgeoning Hudson River seaport. There is a rugged strength to these buildings on Franklin Street, including the granite sidewalks, metal awnings, loading docks, and cobblestone street. The Romanesque Revival style is repeated on the block, where soaring arches frame large sets of windows capped by a single row of smaller windows at the top. What a clever way to break up the façade, an intriguing blend of vertical and horizontal shapes and a design that allows for tons of light inside. Franklin Street is also one of many blocks of TriBeCa, from Duane to Barrow Street, that were laid out perpendicular to the Hudson River in a near true east-west direction. These blocks are off-line with the rest of the city, but they capture light more vibrantly.[1] All the better to show off the architectural richness of color, detail, and materials found on Franklin Street.

Small wonder why Urban Archaeology opened a branch here at #143, a business devoted to the salvage and reproduction of relics of our architectural past. One finds aisles of objects to the ceiling. Scads of out-of-scale items, such as gargantuan clocks, street lamps, and bathtubs are crammed tightly, but elegantly, into the showroom. One feels immersed in the 19th century—no store has a more fluid relationship with the street than this one.

The view east is out of the ordinary toward the "landmark" El Teddy's Restaurant with its Statue of Liberty crown pointing in all directions, but it is the whole vista with water towers and the copper top Deco high-rise on Broadway that makes it special. This block has certainly arrived as an upscale residential and shopping environment, but still retains a bit of working class character. Franklin Street should be carefully studied and savored for its craftsmanship, color, and texture. Perhaps it is not considered cool to stare at the side of building, admiring the stone carving, brickwork, and decorative moldings. But who cares? What's here is too good for a fleeting look.

1. Contrary to a commonly held belief, the cross-island streets of 14th Street and above angle toward the northwest in the direction of Canada, not true west.

FRANKLIN STREET

STAPLE STREET JAY & HARRISON STREETS

Two Points of View

When does an alley become a street? Regardless, Staple is a narrow block with a broad character. At times, it feels more like London, when seen from beneath the arched pedestrian bridge looking toward the majestic Victorian Mercantile Building on Harrison Street. The bridge sets this block apart from all others, with beautifully detailed wainscoting, thin vertical windows, and a copper roof. The east side of the bridge is attached to the rear of 67 Hudson Street, formerly a hospital—the House of Relief Building.[1]

Staple Street is frequently used as a pedestrian passway to the popular and elegantly upscale Duane Street. But it is an alley too; I saw a man urinate against the wall, then enter a building on the block. A bit unusual, were there no facilities inside? Notwithstanding and be careful-where-you-stand, one can still appreciate the rich-

ness of masonry and stonework on the sides of the buildings, along with decoratively intricate iron gates on the windows. These architectural elements plus the layers of paint create the impression of an old Roman street. London, Rome, New York—where are we? On a narrow road, intimate, antiquated, and appreciated by those who love a trace of disorder, old brick, cobblestone, numerous fire escapes, and the sound of one's own footsteps.

A walk down Staple Street encourages two points of view: one from street level with all its details, the other looking down at oneself from above. This out-of-body perception is cultivated by city dwellers who, from overhead, often watch others walk. Split personalities—no, two points of view—are like personal geo-positional coordinates. You know where you are on any street or alley.

1. Harris, Bill, Photographs by Jorg Brockmann. *One Thousand New York Buildings,* New York: Black Dog and Leventhal Publishers, 2002: 110

STAPLE STREET

The Little Building That Could

This stretch of Thomas Street is fascinating because it has so many significant buildings from widely divergent architectural styles. Unfortunately their relationship to the street is like an unsuccessful dinner party where the guests avoid eye contact.

The AT&T Long Lines building dominates Thomas Street at the corner of Church Street. The warm granite facing reflects light beautifully, but the overall effect still frightens people away, as does the adjacent park with its imposing gothic ironwork. To the south side of the street, the 1950s New York State Insurance Fund building is impressive with its sleek wire framework, and a sheer wall of light brick (that is great to photograph), but this building really belongs to Church Street and Trimble Place. Thomas gets the wall.

Walking towards Broadway you pass a line of small and distinctive buildings before reaching the back of a modern apartment building located on Duane Street. Again, we are greeted by a wall, this time the side of #8 Thomas. It is dotted with iron supports that stabilize the building. When I last checked, it was still looking for a buyer, an unusal building that has been characterized as Victorian Gothic,[1] or Romanesque and Venetian Gothic.[2] The way this landmark sits on the street is something out of a children's book—The Little Building That Could. A few steps farther you will reach the side entrance of McDonalds, dwarfed by a great expanse of gray marble. Across the street is the regal white, cast-iron building at 319 Broadway.

There you have it, the oddest collection of buildings in Lower Manhattan, an archipodge block. In the end there are too many empty spaces, set-backs, and sheer walls. Connections are everything to a block, how the buildings touch, and their reasons for being. If you turn and look back towards Church, you can see a history of architecture like chapters in a book.

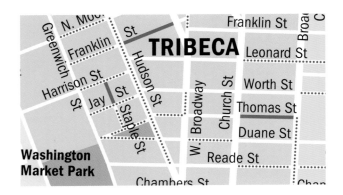

1. Harris, Bill, Photographs by Jorg Brockmann. *One Thousand New York Buildings,* New York: Black Dog and Leventhal Publishers, 2002: 113
2. White, Norval, Elliot Willensky. *AIA Guide to New York City.* New York: Three Rivers Press, 2000: 77

THOMAS STREET

THE CIVIC CENTER, CHINATOWN, & LOWER EAST SIDE

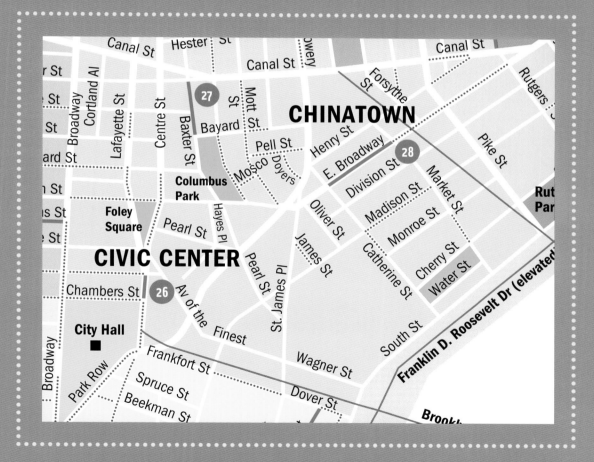

Epicenter Street

In this world where a tall coffee is really a small and advertising distorts the meaning of our language, it is refreshing to find that Centre Street actually is in the center of Lower Manhattan.

This is a one-two block with Manhattan Borough Hall, also known as the Municipal Building, on the east side and the Surrogate's Court on the west. These magnificent public buildings are a credit to the City Beautiful movement at the turn of the 20th century. Greek influence can be seen everywhere—from the massive Corinthian columns to the full figure and relief sculptures. How much drama can be packed into one block? Curious for what may be a side street. The front of Surrogate's Courthouse is on Chambers Street, even the stairway is missing from the side entrance after the 1961[1] widening of the street, and Municipal Hall was built to been seen from a distance preferably from Chambers Street. Everything is on an enormous scale, and as you move from wide-open Foley Square and City Hall, the effect is like being squeezed through an hourglass.

Security barriers have arrived at many of Lower Manhattan's government and corporate buildings, and this is certainly the case on this block. Security needs are a reality that eventually we will learn to incorporate into our lives, but for now it is impossible not to be affected by these images. I recommend that you keep your head up as the real glory is above. Allow the formidable pedestrian traffic of civil service employees to pass by freely. Take the time to look up, and not just for a moment, but long enough to take in the allegorical sculptures.

The intersection of Chambers and Centre Street is a unique site with wonderful sight lines in 360 degrees. Is this the *epicenter* of Manhattan? There seem to be unlimited choices for you to walk, east over the bridge to Brooklyn, west down Chambers, south to stately Park Row, or north past Civic Center into the upper reaches of Manhattan.

1. *Department of Citywide Administrative Services (DCAS) Managed Public Buildings, The Surrogate's Courthouse.* http://www.nyc.gov/html/dcas/html/building/man_surrogatecourt.html

BAXTER STREET BAYARD & CANAL STREETS

Passing Time

Baxter may be *the* crossroads block in all of Lower Manhattan, where many ethnic groups cross paths. This convention of humanity exists in an abundance of architectural contrast that fulfills radically different functions. The basic ingredients include the dominating Deco high-rise Men's House of Detention with its plaza, and Clavin Place, which sits opposite 19th century tenements. Then you add two parking lots, a modern brick residential apartment complex, and storefronts that include an old-fashioned tailor shop, a Chinese art gallery, the Second Chance Bail Bondsman, and a host of restaurants of different nationalities. Whoever gave the Malaysian restaurant, The Marco Polo Noodle, its name hit the nail on the head. A colorful cast of characters, judges, lawyers, guards, police, and other civil servants descend on Baxter for lunch.

It must have been a tremendous shock as each new building was constructed on the west side of Baxter, since the east side has remained mostly 19th century. This kind of old/new split arrangement, or shadow block, normally creates disharmony, but not chez Baxter! Two features on the modern side account for this unintentional success of urban planning: the inviting tree-lined outdoor café, and the short marble-faced wall that was meant as a planter, but now provides a long and desirable place to sit.

Above all things, Baxter serves as a link block, joining both the Civic Center and Little Italy with Chinatown. People pour in from Canal, Bayard, and Clavin Place. A pedestrian pass-through from the west was probably intended to be an open square, but now serves the dual role of a parking lot. Lower Manhattan is filled with great neighborhoods, but they would be isolated islands without important link blocks like Baxter Street.

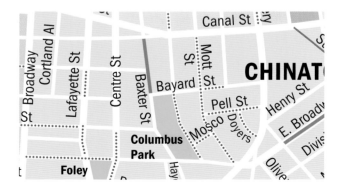

BAXTER STREET

The Other Chinatown

Chinatown is a large and varied locale that continues to grow into the adjoining areas of Little Italy and the Lower East Side. A walk through this neighborhood reveals blocks of many intentions and levels of activity. The Chinatown that tourists and even New Yorkers know best originates from Bayard and Mott Streets. It offers an inviting, but one-sided view, a vivid and densely populated jumble of restaurants and novelty shops. Every conceivable trinket under the sun is offered for sale, a torrent of playfulness that in the end lessens the experience. Chinatown is so much more than that.

East Broadway at Catherine and Market Streets is a service block that provides the neighborhood with shops for vegetables, fish, pharmaceuticals, baked goods, hardware, stationery, videotapes, stationery, shoes, and spices. There is even a strong introspective presence on opposite sides of the street in the magnificent landmark Chatham Square Public Library and in the Grace Gratitude Buddhist Temple. It is busy without being overwhelming—a broad block lined with old box trucks making morning deliveries as the Manhattan

Borough Hall gleams in the distance. This palatial view must have offered some a goal to aspire to and others an image from another world. And, of course, for local residents there is the remembered image of the World Trade Center towers rising in the background.

To the east, the Manhattan Bridge access ramp can be seen just beyond Market Street. The bridge was opened in 1909 as it made its way across the East River, through the Lower East Side slicing many a block in half. These sliced blocks would develop independently of one another, like twins separated at birth. Some of the bridge's enormous gray stone arches have been filled in by the Chinatown equivalent of shopping malls.

East Broadway has a compelling mixture of architecture, an example of how different centuries can coexist, and the unity of the building heights at five and six stories deserves credit for the unusual visual symmetry of the block. At 48 East Broadway, five carved images of Buddha look peacefully out from the window display. Here a fine balance can be sensed throughout on a block from the other Chinatown.

EAST BROADWAY

FULTON, WORLD TRADE CENTER, BATTERY PARK CITY & THE FINANCIAL DISTRICT

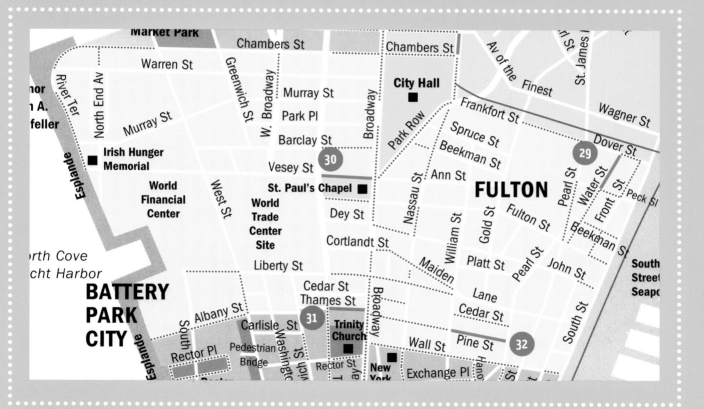

WATER STREET PECK SLIP & DOVER STREET

The Real New York

Water Street once faced the East River, but later found itself two blocks away without a view, as Front and South Streets emerged on landfill. The seaport grew quickly in significance for the city, and it developed a rough reputation. The Bridge Café at #279 has seen it all; it is considered the oldest drinking establishment in New York, since the first mug was poured in 1794. But just imagine later in the 1870s, the working class patrons watched the demolition of the buildings to the north, followed by the slow and incredible construction of the immense Brooklyn Bridge. It was a rude but majestic introduction to the first icon of a modern industrialized world. Water Street, now a dead-end street and literally passed by, depended on an ever-declining seaport. The Fulton Fish Market, however, survived, and many felt this part of Manhattan to be the real New York, warts, bruises, and all.

In the 1960s, the high-rise corporate buildings of the Financial District rapidly advanced northward, destroying the architectural remnants of the 19th century. A large master plan saved the South Street Seaport, but it led to a loss of mystique and a place designed more for tourists than New Yorkers. The area became a historic district in 1977, including this block on Water Street or, more precisely, the east side only. Once on the river's edge, then a dead end, now at risk of being sliced lengthwise, filleted, half-protected from development. Twelve years passed before this error was rectified. Water Street and the immediate area are fine examples of what the South Street Seaport could have been if it had been developed with mixed-use in mind. And to add salt to the wound, Fulton Fish Market is forsaking its boxes of ice for refrigerated new digs in The Bronx.

The Brooklyn Bridge emanates the constant murmur of traffic along with a steady stream of bicyclists and pedestrians. They may get a glimpse of old Water Street, which as always minds its own business, comfortable in the past with roots to the real New York.

WATER STREET

Vital Link

The presence of St. Paul's Chapel and its magnificent trees bring a strong spiritual quality to this block. The events of September 11th would intensify the Chapel's significance beyond anyone's imagination. It served the vital role as a recovery center for the workers and volunteers who labored tirelessly during those desperate days following the destruction of the Twin Towers.

Vesey Street will once again be a vital link block for the World Financial and Trade Center with Broadway/City Hall. Construction is now under away for the Liberty Tower, a new transportation hub,

and Reflecting Absence, the World Trade Center Site Memorial. As one walks west on Vesey Street toward Ground Zero past the long wrought iron fence and St. Paul's cemetery, who can make sense of the hell that happened here?

In the face of tragedy, New Yorkers have always found solace in the promise of the future. The focus and dedication to the redesign of the World Trade Center reflects that long tradition. Yet it is through work and everyday events that New Yorkers rediscover an inspiring sense of purpose and an unwavering tenacity born of many cultures.

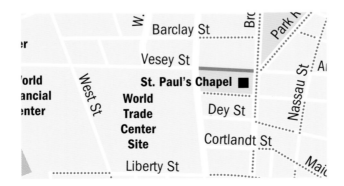

VESEY STREET

Cathedral Thames

Claustrophobics beware, but others may find this block intriguing. Squeezed between two outstanding gothic-inspired skyscrapers, Thames Street is a narrow pedestrian pass-way that provides two restaurants (Suspenders and Big Al's Pizza) with outdoor seating in a sea of white plastic chairs. The U.S. Realty Building, at 115 Broadway to the north and The Trinity Building, 111 Broadway, to the south were both designed by the architect Francis H. Kimball and completed in 1906. The dramatic quality of this block is no mistake, for Kimball was first a prominent theater designer. He was also responsible for the first steel frame skyscraper in New York City, built for the Manhattan Life Insurance Company at 66 Broadway.

As one loses sight of the distant sky, the overall effect on Thames Street is akin to standing inside a great European cathedral. Gargoyles look down from the ornamental detailing of the first two floors that include stained glass, but no pulpit. This sedate block is a poignant reminder, of recent traumatic events, as seen on opposite ends of the street. Trinity Place is eerily quiet, given its close proximity to Ground Zero with an array of buildings still in question. The tall, wrapped Deutsche Bank building is slowly being dismantled. The high side on Broadway is extremely busy with traffic of all kinds in front of the infamous Equitable Building at #120. In 1915, this bulky design, with no setback, created an enormous scandal, and led to an immediate revision to the city building code to prevent future abuses. Unfortunately, the City Council did not anticipate the sheer and foreboding implications of a beckoning international style.

When leaving Thames Street, you should walk downhill and turn left onto Trinity Place. The effect of exiting Cathedral Thames in this way is made even more spiritually significant when you behold the expansive and glorious view of Trinity Church.

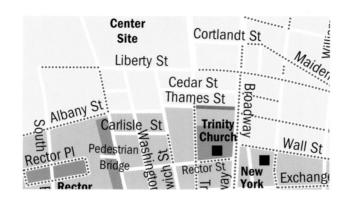

1. Wolfe, Gerard R. *New York, A Guide to the Metropolis.* New York: McGraw Hill, 1988: 9.
2. Eigen, Edward A. "Kimball, Francis." *The Encyclopedia of New York City.* New Haven: Yale University Press, 1995.
3. Wolfe. p. 10

THAMES STREET

32

PINE STREET WILLIAM & PEARL STREETS

Wide Enough

Cigarette smokers from the office caste system, executives, middle management, and mailroom clerks all mingle in front of the office lobbies exchanging a match and an occasional remark. A nota-block on omnipresent Wall Street is just to the south, but Pine Street is no second fiddle. It has a distinctive old Financial District character uniquely its own, sandwiched between a church and a post office. The no-nonsense reality of sidewalk life here is pure New York as it contrasts with the fanciful architecture from decades past.

More than 300 hundred years ago, Pine was laid out as a narrow hilly street barely wide enough to accommodate the needs of the 17th century. Now, with sidewalks five feet wide and a roadway not much greater at 13 feet, it is a miracle that this block allows for the movement of people, goods and services. No city planner today would design an urban street in this way, but thankfully this block has evolved just so.

Pine Street, with its snug east-west alignment, shows off dazzling displays of decorative architecture. The north side is especially impressive and dominated by elaborate entrances and sculptural motifs. Starting on the high side at William Street, there is a succession of architectural gems: Our Lady of Victory, the Caledonia Insurance Company, A.G. Becker & Company, The Cambridge Club, and the American International Building by Pearl Street. When the sun shines, rays of light are present not only from above, but also in the sun motifs at 54 and 70 Pine.

On the south side of the block, you will find the US Post Office and the new Deutsche Bank corporate offices that moved here from Liberty Street after the events of September 11th. Security is overt with camouflage dressed personnel, a poignant contrast to the delicate white latticework interior. The exterior of Deutsche Bank is massive but fashioned in rich marble. On a wider street this bank's size would be overwhelming, but not on Pine. As if in a steep canyon, your eyes look downward to the pedestrians walking among the traffic, then to a view of the East River and Brooklyn beyond.

PINE STREET

THE FINANCIAL DISTRICT
& BATTERY PARK CITY

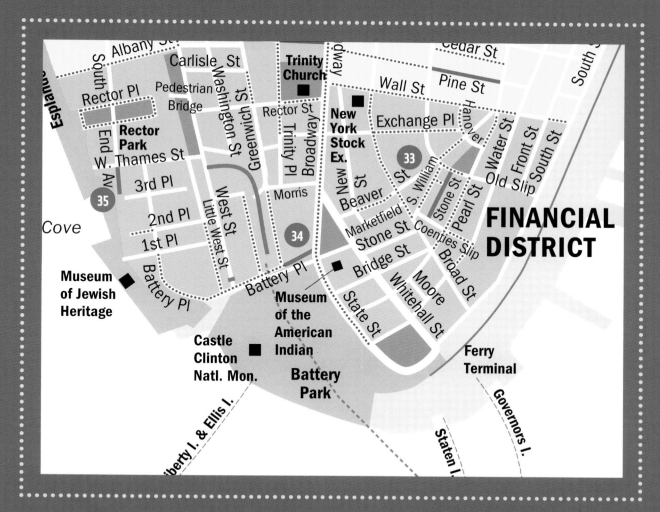

33

STONE STREET   COENTIES ALLEY & WILLIAM STREET

What Took So Long

Deep within the fluorescent confines of Penn Station on West 34th Street, one surprisingly encounters a series of large black and white photographs hung on the square metal columns. These shots describe beautifully the interior and exterior of the former train station. It was a 1910 classically inspired gem revered by all who entered its hallowed doors. This Penn Station truly defined the city as an elegant and pulsating metropolis, yet in 1963, against much opposition, the Pennsylvania Railroad Board of Directors ordered its demise.[1]

Why are the photographs there? Is it a quiet statement of apology for the single worst real estate decision in New York City history? If so, small consolation, but it did spark the preservation movement and the founding of the New York City Landmarks Preservation Commission. Some 80 historical districts are now designated throughout the city, 17 in Lower Manhattan, including Stone Street. However, it is still a miracle that this block survives in its present state. In 1983, the construction of an office tower at #85 Broad Street at the end of Coenties

Alley sliced the four-century-old Stone Street in half. It took three decades to establish historic district protection for this block in 1996, which has since been restored and is now lined with restaurants.

Stone Street rose from the ashes of the 1835 fire that destroyed 674 buildings along the seaport, including most of the remaining structures from the Dutch colony. This devastating event seemed only to accelerate the growth of the area, with 500 buildings completed within a year. This time, on wider and straighter streets, only commercial structures with fire resistant brick and granite were built. It was now the Financial District that would propel the city to prominence.[2]

Stone Street is well known and fittingly named, since it was the first paved street in all of New Amsterdam. That momentous event took three decades from the inception of the colony. Many must have greeted this stone-street improvement as a revelation, a bold proclamation that the colony was here to stay. Other New Amsterdamers probably wondered what took so long.

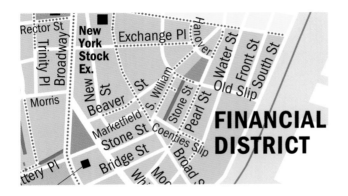

FINANCIAL DISTRICT

1. The epitaph no one wants: instead of photographs, why not hang a plaque, "In 1963, the following Board of Directors voted to demolish Pennsylvania Station, a NYC architectural treasure."
2. Burrows, Edwin G., Mike Wallace, *Gotham: A History of New York City to 1898.* New York: Oxford University Press, 1999: 596-599

STONE STREET

The First New Yorker

Who would have predicted that from this spot the greatest city in the world would arise? Perhaps it was a given, considering the remarkable orientation of the harbor with two rivers framing this long point of land. It is an understatement to say that it made a good port, and with the spot came spirituality inherent in the seascape.

The city began here in 1625, yet nearly everything has changed. No architecture remains from the 17th century, and very little from the 18th. Fort Amsterdam is long gone, and landfill has significantly altered the shape of the Lower Manhattan. The Hudson River was just a block west, and many of the original hills are now flat. What remains is essential: Bowling Green, the city's first park, the land containing Battery Park, and the original layout for the surrounding streets. Anyone trying to imagine what New Amsterdam once was like need only observe the natural elements, the interplay of light and water that graces Battery Place with a special ambience.

Peter Stuyvesant, as the newly appointed Director General of New Netherland, arrived in 1647 charged with restoring order to the colony after years of mismanagement. He would govern New Amsterdam until the British ousted the Dutch in 1664. Peter Stuyvesant is certainly the first of the many larger-than-life characters to inhabit this city. After a short stay in The Netherlands, he returned, preferring to spend the rest of his days as a New Yorker, even though it meant living under British rule.

A single building, the side of 1 Broadway, occupies this park block. Here stands the majestic United States Lines-Panama Pacific Lines Building, once headquarters to the famous passenger ship companies. This notable structure was built in 1921 on the most appropriate spot conceivable, but herein lies a missed opportunity. The main entrance should really have been designed for Battery Place facing the park and the harbor. But a Broadway address was just too seductive. Interestingly, the two small side entrances are for first and cabin-class passengers, with first-class situated closer to Broadway, of course.

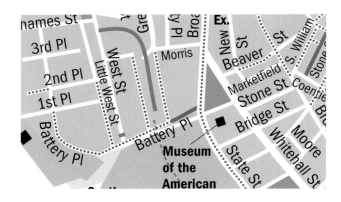

BATTERY PLACE

35

SOUTH END AVENUE   SOUTH COVE PARK & WEST THAMES STREET

Getting it Right

This block in Battery Park City was created in the late 1970s. In thirty years the trees have matured, the buildings have weathered, and the overall plan has settled in. The streets are lined with modern brick apartments with arcades that give protection from the elements in what is often misty weather. This row of columns is most attractive from the street, but the interior of the arcade feels sterile and lacks the decorative features necessary to soften the weight of the columns. In this Roman-inspired environment, the dry cleaner looks out of place. If only they could hang the shirts outside. Also, there are long stretches toward West Thames Street with dark windows of nothingness except one's own reflection. The original architects and urban planners certainly had something more in mind. Could it be that the residents here have automobiles to use to go shop elsewhere?

Perhaps you were thinking South End Avenue would be longer, more of a thoroughfare, but at 1/3 of a mile it seems more a street or a lane. If West Street can be a street, then so can South End. Exaggeration is great for real estate sales but diminishes our language. Nevertheless, this stretch of road ends with a cul de sac and South Cove Park, and here you will find one of the most stunning views in all of Lower Manhattan. The open space perfectly frames Ellis Island and the Statue of Liberty. The Museum of Jewish Heritage with its Star of David shaped design is just to the south. Lower Manhattan, acutely short of parks, now has South Cove Park, the Esplanade, and Robert Wagner Park, all beautifully designed, implemented, and maintained. The influence of Frederick Olmstead via Central Park is unmistakable. New York City has always been appreciated through film taken from passenger ships entering the harbor. Now, surrounded by trees, one looks out over the water and open sky with the equally vast city envisioned at your back.

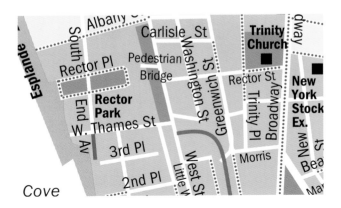

SOUTH END AVENUE

36

Could Have Been Street

Manhattan *Avenue* is easily located on any New York City map between 100th and 125th Streets, but no amount of searching will turn up Manhattan Street. Make no mistake, it truly lies in Lower Manhattan. Unless of course, the large block letters that spell out its name on the side of a building are an elaborate ruse. Exactly where it is will be discovered only by the most curious of blockologists, for Manhattan Street is no more than a glorified driveway, a non-block.

Why did such a distinguished street name shrivel in insignificance to be completely overshadowed by an avenue far to the north and years later? Manhattan Street deserved a better fate; it rolls right off the tongue with visions of a long and distinguished thoroughfare, a rival to Broadway. And who was present when both East and West Broadway were unimaginatively titled in a transparent attempt to inflate real estate values? Did anyone suggest Manhattan Street?

The Commissioners' Plan of 1811 that laid out the grid pattern for the whole island could have easily mandated Houstoun Street to henceforth be proclaimed as Manhattan Street. No offence to William Houstoun, the patriot from aristocratic Georgian stock, but he received this honor through marriage not deed, and it has been a troublesome cognomen ever since.[1] Even the spelling somehow got changed to Houston. It is a New Yorker's secret delight to set Texans straight. "You say HUEston, we say HOWston!" No amount of explanations will ever suffice. For what reason do we perpetuate this north/south confrontation? Provincialism?

In the end, what is done is done. Manhattan Street can be found in its current state, east of West Broadway, north of East Broadway, while walking east on the north side of North Street, now known by another name.

1. Moscow, Henry. *The Street Book: An Encyclopedia of Manhattan's Street Names and Their Origins*, New York: Fordham University Press, 1978: 61

MANHATTAN STREET

GLOSSARY

The blocks of Lower Manhattan are engaging for their endless variety. Each block is uniquely complex as to its purpose, design, and interconnection to the city. Blocks reveal themselves well when observed through the context of continuity (similarities in purpose and appearance), contrast (disparity, variety, and comparison), and character (personality and background). The following terms are but a small sample of the patterns and conditions that exist, for a block can be seen and described in many ways.

ARCHIPODGE BLOCK: A block that has no two buildings with the same architectural style.

BACK BLOCK: The backside of a prominent block, which dominates or strongly influences its character.

BINDER BLOCK: A large number of educational buildings that creates an urban campus on a block.

BLUR BLOCK: Serves the city for the free movement of cars with multiple lanes and timed lights. The block is a blur to both drivers and pedestrians.

BORDER BLOCK: A block that takes on the character of two neighborhoods.

CARGO BLOCK: A block with mostly warehouses and or storage centers.

CELLBLOCK: Newly developed in a manner that disregards the original architecture and building materials. Any similarity to prison architecture is intentional.

CENTURY BLOCK: Two distinct styles of architecture that face each on opposite sides of the street. This often refers to 19th versus 20th century. One of the great ironies in real estate is that the most visually offensive property has the better view.

CHAT BLOCK: Where a large number of people stand and talk. Chat blocks are common in Lower Manhattan, as neighbors get to know each other better, which makes urban life so agreeable.

CHOPPED BLOCK: Renovated, bricked, and painted to distraction for short-term gain and long-term loss to the neighborhood. These blocks can reclaim their former glory as long as the original buildings have not been torn down.

CLEAR BLOCK: No trees. Not always a negative condition as some city blocks especially on Broadway, do well without them.

CLOISTER BLOCK: Hard to find, often because of the maze-like pattern of intersecting streets that create odd angles and dead ends. These blocks live peacefully in the shadow of easy-to-find blocks.

COMMUNITY BLOCK: A balance in the retail mix meets both the needs of the neighborhood with essential services (service block) and of the greater community with restaurants and shops that have broader appeal.

CROSSROADS BLOCK: A block that marks the coming together of two or more distinct cultures in population and retail storefronts.

DOCK BLOCK: A large amount of loading docks that are *still* in use. The architects for high-rises in the early 20th century utilized architectural details and motifs in their loading docks, in a noble attempt to disguise back from front.

FILE BLOCK: Offices only.

GO BLOCK: A block that is always active with walkers moving at a set rate, otherwise known as a pedestrian freeway.

GUEST BLOCK Where only tourists tend to gather. The character of a guest block resembles a theme park or mall corridor. The architecture, regardless of how significant, exists merely for the pleasure of those guests, who as pedestrians are first and foremost customers on foot.

GUT BLOCK: A block that changes every time you look with new renovations, residents, and retail as a result of an encroaching neighborhood or new development.

ITEM BLOCK: Shops on a single block that sell the same kind of product or merchandise. This can run the gamut from restaurant equipment to lighting fixtures.

LAG BLOCK: Where large parcels of property are stagnated in the endless promise of development, and buildings are left in disrepair, surrounded in scaffolding or fenced in.

LEAF BLOCK: A great many trees lining both sides of the block, which can include planters and crawling vines.

LINK BLOCK: Connects two prominent blocks or two neighborhoods.

LOT BLOCK: Lots of parking lots. In the 19th century, these were called stable blocks with a distinct aroma.

MARKET BLOCK: A block lined with produce stands, either in storefronts or by way of farmer's markets.

MENU BLOCK: Restaurants and cafes occupy most of the storefronts.

MIRROR BLOCK: A single architectural style prevails on both sides of the street.

MOAT BLOCK: Wealthy residents on one side of the street and poor on the other.

MODTOP BLOCK: A block where modern additions, penthouse-like, have been constructed on top of older buildings.

MONOLOG BLOCK: A block with only one tree. The tree can range from a sapling clinging to life that tears at your heartstrings to a fully mature tree that seems to own the block. In either case, the tree's isolation suggests a story. Who planted and cared for it?

NOTA-BLOCK: A notable block, often with a landmark.

ONE-TWO BLOCK: One building on each side of the street.

PARK BLOCK: A park on one side of the street and buildings on the other.

PORTAL BLOCK: The entrance to a neighborhood. Neighborhoods do not have walls around them, so there are many ways to enter; nonetheless, a single block will claim that right.

PUFF BLOCK: Where smoking in front of buildings is commonplace.

RALLY BLOCK: A great many people stand, talk, drink, smoke, and carry on.

REC-BLOCK: A block with a large playground.

RES-BLOCK: Residential buildings only, no retail stores at all.

SALT BLOCK: A block that captures the spice of the neighborhood.

SERVICE BLOCK: A block that serves only the local neighborhood with a variety of shops, such as groceries, hardware stores, laundries, and dry cleaners.

SHADOW BLOCK: Tall buildings on one side of the street and small buildings on the other.

SHOW BLOCK: Where a large number of entertainment venues, theaters, and clubs.

SHRINE BLOCK: A block with a large number of spiritual institutions, such as churches, mosques, temples, and synagogues. Libraries also add to this contemplative atmosphere.

SLICED BLOCK: A block divided by an access road or bridge ramp. This creates two blocks out of one, and the two halves develop independently of each other.

SPLIT LEAF BLOCK: Trees on one side of the street and none on the other.

STEP BLOCK: A block of front stoops.

TAG BLOCK: Shops with window displays fill all or most of the storefronts.

UNICUISINE BLOCK: All of the restaurants and cafes offer the same cuisine.

VISOR BLOCK: A block dominated by modern apartment buildings where all the resources in decorative materials and design have been spent on exterior of the first one or two floors and none thereafter. New York City made its reputation looking up; now often caps are required.

INDEX

NEAREST SUBWAY GUIDE

Blocks	Subway Stations/Trains
West Village & Greenwich Village	
Ganesvoort Street Greenwich & Hudson Streets	14th St. @ 8th Ave. **A,C,E,L**
	Christopher St.-Sheridan Sq. @ 7th Ave South. **1,2**
Bedford Street Barrow & Grove Streets	Christopher St.-Sheridan Sq. @ 7th Ave South. **1,2**
St. Luke's Place Hudson & Seventh Avenue South	Houston St. @ Varick (7th Ave. South) **1,2**
Washington Place South Sullivan & Thompson Streets	W. 4th St.-Washington Sq. @ 6th Ave. **A,B,C,F,S,V**
East 11th Street University Place & Broadway	8th St. @ Broadway **N,R,**
	14th St.-Union Sq. @4th Ave. **4,6,L,N,Q,R,W**
NoHo & East Village	
Great Jones Street Lafayette Street & Bowery	Bleecker St. @ Lafayette St. **6**
First Avenue East 1st & 2nd Streets	Lower East Side/2nd Ave. & 1st Ave.@ Houston St. **F,V**
Second Avenue East 7th Street & St. Mark's Place	Astor Place @ 8th St. & 4th Ave. **6**
East 10th Street Avenues A & B	1st Ave. @ 14th St. **L**
Avenue C East 8th & 9th Streets	1st Ave. @ 14th St. **L**
Lower East Side	
Clinton Street Stanton & East Houston Streets	Lower East Side/2nd Ave. & 1st Ave. @ Houston St. **F,V**
	Bowery @ Delancey St. **J,M**
Orchard Street Delancey & Rivington Streets	Lower East Side/2nd Ave. & 1st Ave. @ Houston St. **F,V**
	Delancey St. @ Essex St. **F**
Henry Street Montgomery & Grand Streets	East Broadway @ Rutgers St. **F**
Essex Street Canal & Hester Streets	East Broadway @ Rutgers St. **F**
Little Italy, NoLita, & the Bowery	
Mulberry Street Hester & Grand Street	Canal St. @ Centre St. **J**
	Canal St. @Lafayette St. **6**
	Canal St. @ Broadway **N,Q**
Elizabeth Street Prince & East Houston Streets	Broadway-Lafayette St, @ Houston St. **F,V**
	Bleecker St. @Lafayette St. **6**
Broadway Grand & Broome Streets	Canal St. @Broadway **N,Q**
	Spring St. @Lafayette St. **6**

SoHo and Hudson Square

Greene Street Broome & Spring Streets

Sullivan Street Prince & West Houston Streets
Spring Street Washington & Greenwich Streets

Broadway-Lafayette St, @ Houston St. **F,V**
Spring St. @ Lafayette St. **6**
Spring St. @ 6th Ave. **C,E**
Spring St. @ 6th Ave. **C,E**
Houston St. @ Varick (7th Ave. South) **1,2**

TriBeCa

Ericsson Street Hudson & Varick Streets

Franklin Street Hudson & Varick Streets
Staple Street Jay & Harrison Streets

Thomas Street Church Street & Broadway

Canal St. @ Varick St. **1,2**
Canal St. @ 6th Ave. **A, E**
Franklin St. @ Varick St. **1,2**
Franklin St. @ Varick St. **1,2**
Chambers St. @ West Broadway **1,2**
Chamber St. @ Church St. **A,C**
Brooklyn Bridge-City Hall @Centre St. **4,5,6,J,Z**

The Civic Center Chinatown, & Lower East Side

Centre Street Chambers & Reade Streets
Baxter Street Bayard & Canal Streets

East Broadway Catherine & Market Streets

Brooklyn Bridge-City Hall @ Centre St. **4,5,6,J,Z**
Canal St. @ Centre St. **J,M,Z**
Canal St. @ Lafayette St. **6**
Brooklyn Bridge, City Hall @ Centre St. **4,6,J,Z**

Fulton, World Trade Center, Battery Park City & the Financial District

Water Street Peck Slip & Dover Street
Vesey Street Church Street & Broadway

Thames Street Trinity Place & Broadway
Pine Street William & Pearl Streets

Fulton St. @ William St. **1,2**
World Trade Center @ Church St. **E**
Park Place @ Broadway **1,2**
Wall St. @ Broadway **4,5**
Wall St. @ William St. **1,2**

The Financial District & Battery Park City

Stone Street Coenties Alley & William Street

Battery Place Greenwich Street & Broadway
South End Avenue South Cove Park & West Thames Street

Wall St. @ William St. **1,2**
Bowling Green @ Broadway **4,5**
Bowling Green @ Broadway **4,5**
Bowling Green @ Broadway **4,5**

NOTES